Puppy Life Skills

ISBN: 9798403396691
Beta readers: Kristin Lucey, and Lisadawn Shackleford

DOG INSPIRED

Puppy
Life Skills

Katherine Davidson

A guide to helping you raise a happy puppy.

TERMINOLOGY

Pronouns: I use the pronouns "them" or "their" when talking about animals or people. I often use "puppy" or "dog" as a general term.

Human-dog relationship: I do not like the term "dog owner". I don't believe that we own dogs or animals are objects, but are instead sentient beings. Therefore, I choose to use the term "pet parent" or "pet guardian". While this may not reflect each individual relationship that each person has with their dog, they are the terms I feel most comfortable using.

Results disclaimer: It's important to note that guarantees do not exist in dog training. It is also highly unethical to make such claims. If any dog professional guarantees results, they are not being transparent about their work.

In this book, I put every effort into providing information on behaviour and training that is humane but also effective. The training plans have been well vetted and used on hundreds of dogs. Note that results depend on various factors including your puppy's learning curve, motivation, your management strategies, consistencies and time practiced on the exercises.

Medical advice: I am not a veterinarian or professional in animal health. Therefore, I do not make any recommendations when it comes to food, diet or health.

Any sudden change in your puppy's behaviour needs to be assessed by your veterinary team.

DEDICATED TO

Harlow, my forever puppy. You have been the best teacher and partner in my dog training journey. I am forever grateful for all the important lessons you have taught me over the years. You kept me on my toes, always. Thank you for making me better.

To my daughter, Lily. You inspire me.

To my loving and incredibly supportive husband Corey. Without you, I don't think any of this would be possible. You make sure I'm well fed, you look over my work and you listen to me go off on tangents about dogs. Thank you for everything you do for me.

WELCOME

Congratulations on the addition of your new family member! Bringing home a new puppy is always so exciting, and maybe a bit nerve wracking! You are about to embark on a 10-15 year commitment; a big life decision!

My passion for puppy training has come from my experience working in shelters. I saw so many young dogs being relinquished due to "rowdy", jumpy and mouthy behaviours. Many of these behaviours are preventable with proper socialization, management and training during the early months after adoption.

Trust me when I say, I've been there. Harlow was a handful. Even working as a dog trainer, I struggled. There is so much I wish I had done to help us be better prepared for his adolescence. This is why I am extending my knowledge and experience on to you. My goal with puppy training is to help you raise a happy, confident puppy and live a long and happy life together.

I am a graduate from Jean Donaldson's Academy for Dog Trainers, a certified Puppy Start Right Instructor from the Karen Pryor Academy and a certified separation anxiety trainer. I have spent a good part of the last 8 years gaining as much knowledge as I can from the industry's best, while gaining hands-on experience with private clients, group classes at a local kennel club and working in shelters.

Katherine Davidson

VISION & MISSION

My mission with Dog Inspired is to inspire today's pet parents through **education** and **compassion**. I am committed to helping new puppy parents raise their puppy using humane and science based methods.

> Properly used, positive reinforcement is extremely powerful.

- B.F Skinner

The methods and ideas used in this book are all based on positive reinforcement. Research has shown both that using positive reinforcement is just as effective as other methods and that using solely positive reinforcement decreases unwanted behaviours!

CONTENTS

01

Before bringing home your puppy

Picking your puppy...............................14

Puppy proofing...................................19

Bringing puppy home...................20

Car safety........…....................…........22

First night home...............................23

Introducing other pets...................26

Introducing children.......................28

House rules myths............................30

List of essentials..............................31

02

Raising a happy, confident puppy

Socialization..36

Dog body language.............................37

Creating positive experiences...........38

Puppy play skills.................................40

Checklist..44

30 day socialization challenge.........45

03

The essential puppy life skills

Training concepts............................50

Body handling.................................52

Resource guarding..........................54

Coming when called.......................55

Leash skills....................................58

Stay on a mat.................................60

Leave it...61

04

Creating good habits early

Normal dog behaviours.....................68

Management....................................69

Enrichment......................................70

Prevention unwanted behaviours........74

Using new skills...............................74

05

Puppy biting

What's normal?................................82

Fearful biting...................................83

Play biting.......................................84

Playing with your puppy....................88

06

House training

Myths...94

Appropriate potty area...................95

Extra potty details..............................96

Handling messes.................................98

The protocol..99

07

Alone time training

Myths...106

Alone time space..................................108

Crate training.......................................110

Alone time training..............................112

Separation anxiety...............................115

Alone time checklist............................117

NOTES

CHAPTER
ONE

Before Bringing Home Puppy
How to pick a puppy, list of essentials and puppy proofing your home.

Picking your puppy

Bringing home a puppy is a big decision and a 10-15 year commitment. This is why we often stress the importance of choosing the right breed and the right breeder.

Here are a few things to consider:

Grooming needs: Some breeds require more grooming. We still need to clean their eyes, cut their nails and give them baths. Some will require daily brushing! Think poodles and all the varieties, and long hair dogs.

Energy levels: Not all dogs are "built" the same. Looking up your potential puppy's breed will help you learn how to care for them. Some breeds require much more exercise than others. High energy dogs include Vizslas, German Shorthaired Pointers, and Weimaraner. These dogs require heavy daily exercise.

Temperament: Dogs are bred for specific jobs. Dogs bred to be "protective" can be spooky with strangers and need a lot of socialization to prevent stranger danger.

Once you have made the choice amongst breeds, it's time to look into where you can acquire your new best friend. Not all breeders are the same. So here are a few questions to ask when enquiring about a puppy:

- How old will the puppy be when you pick them up? (Should not be younger than 8 weeks old!)
- What is the character and temperament of the parents?
- Can you meet the parents?
- Where is the puppy being kept?
- What socialization program do they use?
- Have there been any specific health or behaviour issues from past litters?

Dog Breeds

Golden Retriever

Size: 55-75lbs
Grooming: Medium long coat, lots of shedding
Energy: Easily motivated to learn, requires daily exercise and mental stimulation

Character: Friendly and playful

German Shorthaired Pointer

Size: 45-70lbs
Grooming: Short coat with moderate shedding
Energy: Easily motivated to learn, very high energy requiring considerable physical and mental exercise
Character: Friendly and playful

Cavalier King Charles

Size: 13-18lbs
Grooming: Medium silky coat, low shedding
Energy: Easily motivated to learn, requires moderate exercise and mental stimulation
Character: Friendly and affectionate

German Shepherd

Size: 65-90lbs
Grooming: Long double coat, lots of shedding
Energy: Easily motivated to learn, high energy requiring daily physical and mental exercise
Character: "Protective", "reserved"

After looking at the breeds on the previous page, we see that not all dogs are "built" the same way. This is true for size, personality and energy.

When we talk about energy, we mean that some dogs were bred for a specific task. You might notice certain behaviours in certain breeds.

For example:
German Shepherds are bred to be watch dogs. They tend to bark and be unapproachable by strangers. This means socialization is a high priority for these types of dogs.

German Shorthaired Pointers are bred for hunting. They are known for speed, agility and endurance. You can imagine that a short walk in the morning and at night will not be enough for this type of dog. Adequate daily physical and mental exercise is needed to keep these pups happy.

Poodles and the mixes come in a variety of sizes. While they don't all shed, they require daily brushings to keep their coat free from mats and knots. Poodles are also bred for hunting and require more daily exercise than the average dog.

Let's say your puppy is a mixed breed (intended or from a rescue); it is a myth that mixed breed dogs are healthier, physically or mentally. Genetics are still present and your pup may acquire health or behaviour issues from any breeds they are mixed with.

It's also impossible to say which breed characteristics your pup will obtain from their genetics when mixed. Purebred dogs should be bred for the best health physically, and bred with no behaviour issues.

Behaviour issues such as fear and aggression have a strong genetic component. Resource guarding, stranger aggression and separation anxiety mostly come from your puppy's genetics. This is why it's so important to ask about behaviour history.

Here's the thing: most of us didn't know what to ask or were unaware of how breeding should be done and that's okay. We know more for the future and for now, we can do what we can to help our puppy be well prepared for their life with us by:

- focusing on socialization
- practicing life skills
- and preventing behaviours unwanted

4 BREEDER RED FLAGS

01 You cannot meet the parents. The parents are a reflection of your puppy's future character.

02 Puppies live in a barn, shed or outside. They did not receive any socialization and the environment is unkept and barren.

03 Puppy is less than 8 weeks old when you pick them up. (However, some breeders do lie about this)

04 They cannot give you any health or behavioural information about past litters. They don't provide vaccination records.

There are a variety of places to acquire a puppy including:

- A breeder
- A family whose dog had a litter; or
- A shelter or rescue.

What can breeders and shelters do to help set their puppies up for success?

- Implement a thorough socialization program
- Begin housetraining
- Practice body handling and grooming
- Begin teaching life skills
- Interview potential adopters to find the best match for their puppies

One thing is for certain: we need to start holding breeders to a higher standard in order to see the changes we want to see.

If your puppy is coming from a shelter or a rescue, it is vital that the puppies are born and raised in a calm, stress-free environment.

There should be a socialization program put in place to help prepare the puppies for their future. I have personally helped raise puppies in a shelter setting. I created a thorough socialization program that included introducing people, animals, smells, sounds, textures, grooming and even basic training.

Implementing these socialization strategies is totally possible when a shelter has volunteers. Everyone is running to come play with the puppies!

Puppy Proofing Your Home

There are a few things that should get done before puppy comes home. Setting up their space will help with creating good habits early, and prevent unwanted behaviours.

Here is a checklist to help guide you through the process:

1) Hide/remove loose wires. If you have wires under a TV stand or couch, keep in mind that small puppies can wiggle themselves into small spaces. You might want to put up a barrier like a garden fence to block access.

2) Put knickknacks away. Puppies tend to knock stuff off of tables, which can break or be a potential chew toy.

3) Place plants (especially those toxic to animals) higher up. Consider using hanging macramé for your plants to keep them off the ground.

4) Hide garbage cans. Keep them high up or put them away in a cupboard. Dogs love to forage. I can almost guarantee that they will seek out the garbage if it's left out.

5) Block access to bedrooms using gates. Bedrooms are full of stuff including shoes, clothing, kids toys and other personal items. Many dogs, including my own, ingest dirty underwear and socks. The best thing to do is prevent access to these spaces.

6) Keep countertops and tables clean, and free from food. Remember, dogs love to forage. We will talk more about this in the next chapters.

Bringing Puppy Home

The most exciting part is finally bringing puppy home. The next page discusses car safety in more detail. You should give it a read before picking up your puppy.

When you pick up your puppy, you need to bring with you:
- A 6ft leash
- A collar
- A blanket
- Yummy treats
- Food and water (if you are traveling far)
- A crate (if this is how you choose to transport puppy - see next page)

These items are easily forgotten (I didn't bring anything when I picked up Harlow!) but they can make the ride a little more comfortable for everyone. The collar and leash don't need to be fancy or expensive. Keep in mind puppies will outgrow their collars pretty quickly!

The treats will help make a positive first impression! Giving puppy a treat whenever they come up to you will add lots of value to your relationship!

If you will be travelling far, remember to bring puppy to pee before leaving, and stop every few hours for a potty break. Bring food and water for the journey home!

The First Meeting

It easy to get really excited and squeaky when we first meet our new puppy. Keep in mind that this can be pretty overwhelming. Ideally, sit down to get to puppy's eye level. Be soft and gentle in your interactions. Bring the treats and feed your puppy whenever they come up to you and interact with your family. Read the body language page to learn more about how to understand signs of stress and manage your interactions as needed.

Arriving Home

Take puppy out to their potty area before going inside. Give them some time to explore and sniff. If they pee or poo, give a tasty treat then go inside.

Your puppy will want to explore. It's okay for them to do so as long as they are being supervised. Keep a close eye to redirect your puppy if they start to bite or chew anything. Provide them access to their safe space to go settle down such as a bed, crate or play pen. Make water, toys and food accessible.

By the time puppy comes home, you should have already started to puppy proof. However, there might be a few things you missed! This is why it's important to supervise your puppy. Remove any objects that can be dangerous or easily broken. Use gates and close doors as needed.

Car Safety

Bringing puppy home is so exciting! This section will help you prepare for the ride home, and make car rides safe and fun for them.

Harness or crate:

Anything that is not tied down in a car has a potential to be a projectile if there is a crash. This is super dangerous for your dog, but also for you and your family.

A crash protection harness that is securely fastened with a seat belt is an excellent choice. Centre for Pet Safety (CPS) is an excellent resource to find the best fitting harness for your puppy.

Next, a crate that is strapped down or a carrier placed on the floor behind a seat can be a good alternative to the harness.

Letting your puppy stick their head out the window might look fun, but debris that goes into their ears and eyes can be painful.

Potential messes:

Keep in mind that you are bringing home a puppy that probably cannot handle a long car ride. Frequent potty breaks will be needed on longer trips.

However, I suggest you be prepared for any mess that might happen:

- Waterproof car hammock Paper towel
- Disinfectant spray
- Poo bags
- Small garbage bags Water based wipes

If your puppy pees or vomits in the car, even if you just brought them out, please know they did not do this on purpose. The best thing is to safely pull over, and clean up the mess.

Car sickness:

A lot of dogs struggle with car motion sickness. Talk to your veterinarian for their recommended products to help ease your puppy's nausea.

If your puppy has a hard time in the car, some training will be necessary to get them to gradually be more comfortable in conjunction with medication from your veterinarian.

If it's not addressed, your puppy can create a negative association to the car from being sick!

Puppy's First Night

MYTH: Puppies need to be crated at bedtime.

Nope! You can crate your puppy but only if this is something that works better for you! Everyone has an opinion about this, which can be quite confusing as a new puppy parent. I've personally done it both ways. I much prefer to bed share initially then transition to another space as needed.

Management and supervision:

If puppy will have space to roam at night, whether it's in your room or another space, we need to make sure the space has been properly puppy proofed. We want to remove anything that can be chewed or can be broken.

Keep in mind that potty accidents will happen, so you may consider providing a potty area for bed time.

Nighttime Potty Breaks:

Puppies have tiny bladders, therefore night time potty breaks may be required for the first few weeks. You might not actually need them at all. Every puppy is different!

Preventative measures are always a good idea. You may want to set up an indoor potty area if your puppy is in a room or even in their crate. You can also set an alarm on your phone to wake up in the middle of the night to bring them out to pee. Remember, this is not forever. Even though it may seem like it at 3 in the morning.

Puppy might be very awake after going outside; you can give them something to keep them busy for a while until they fall asleep. A bully stick, a stuffed kong or any other chew toy can do the trick. You will soon find a good night time routine together that will let you both get the rest you need.

If your puppy is peeing multiple times a night, or has diarrhea, consult your veterinary team as there may be an underlying health issue.

I do not suggest withholding water from puppies, but if you have any concern, you can ask your veterinary team.

Bedtime:

There is no right or wrong way to do this. You have to go with what feels right for you and your family. Here are a few ways to navigate bedtime:

Bed sharing:
Letting your puppy sleep in your bed with you is perfectly acceptable. You will probably get a better night sleep than if you use a crate.

If bed sharing no longer works for you, you can change it. During my pregnancy, I transitioned Harlow's sleep space from our room to the living room. He still sleeps there today! It takes patience and going gradually, but it can be done!

Crate or play pen
If you opt out of bed sharing, you might consider a crate or play pen. This is a good strategy to manage your puppy. Keep in mind that puppies chew and most are not house trained yet.

I suggest having the crate in your bedroom, and eventually transitioning to another space if that is what you prefer.

Keep in mind that your puppy has never slept alone before.

Sleeping alone in a crate with no one around can be extremely distressing. This is why I suggest bed sharing or having the crate in your room.

Night time crate/playpen should include:
• Potty area Bed/blanket
• Water
• A toy or bone to chew

Puppy Crying:

If your puppy is in their crate or in another room, they will probably cry. Remember, they have never slept alone before.

A few minutes of small whines or cries is very normal. However, howling and crying for hours is a huge red flag!

Some puppies may settle down and "self soothe"; most do not. The first few nights, you might end up trying a few different bed time set ups until you find something that works best for you.

Having the crate in your room might be the best step-up and you may choose to gradually transition them to a different space as needed.

Introducing Other Pets

Introducing Dogs:

When introducing a new puppy to your current fur kids, keep in mind that they might not tolerate the puppy all that well. Puppies are very energetic, and mouthy.

We want the first introductions to be short and positive. Keep an eye out for signs of stress in your dogs' body language, and manage the interactions closely.

If your dog growls or snaps at your new puppy, know that this is completely normal. Don't punish the growl. Instead, put puppy on leash or behind a gate.

Take lots of breaks. Let them investigate each other from opposite sides of a gate and use food to reward good behaviours in both your dog and puppy such as:

- Sniffing
- Offering play signals (see page 40)
- Looking at each other
- Looking away
- Laying down/sitting

Slow and steady wins the race. This statement is just as true when we introduce our puppy to their new housemates.

Introducing Cats:

Just like with other dogs, we will want to go slowly with the first interactions. Keep them short and sweet. To ensure a more positive experience for both the puppy and your cat, here are a few tips:

- Keep puppy on leash so they can't chase the cat
- Have baby gates set up
- Provide your cat with a space that is a puppy free zone
- Keep interactions short (a few minutes at a time at most)

- Reward your puppy when:
    - They sit or lay down in the presence of the cat
    - When they look at the cat
    - When they look away from the cat
- Reward your cat for being in the room, being curious and give treats simply to help them create positive associations too!

Cat introductions should go much more slowly then with dogs. We want to prevent puppy from chasing and wrestling with the cat. Use the leash and gates. Don't worry, it won't be forever. The time you spend making everyone feel safe will pay off in the long run!

Introducing Children:

Children under 12 years old and dogs need to be tightly managed and supervised. Children can be loud, impulsive and rough. Puppies are no exception; they jump and bite and this will be difficult for a child to manage.

Babies and toddlers

To ensure everyone's safety, management needs to be the first priority. Baby gates are a must, and using play pens is also another suitable management option.

An adult should always be between a toddler and a dog (of any age). Babies cannot read when a dog is uncomfortable. The fact that they are often face level to the dog increases a child's risk of being bitten.

While we may trust our dog or puppy, it's best to stay on the side of caution. Accidents happen but we don't want them to happen to our children.

Don't let baby approach when puppy is sleeping or eating
Avoid interactions that "corners" a dog (dog is on the couch, under a table, in a corner...)

Do not let puppy/dog sniff baby's face
Always have an adult between the baby and dog/puppy

First introductions

Have your older children sit on the floor. Instruct them to stay calm and use a quiet voice to not overwhelm the puppy.

Children will need a lot of coaching and repetition when it comes to interacting with the puppy.

If puppy is happy to greet the children, they can pet the puppy on their chest or shoulder. Avoid patting on the head and hugging the puppy. Remember, this will take a lot of repeating for your children to remember.

If puppy wants to play, have the children use a toy such as fetching with a ball or toy.

Practice consent tests with the puppy. Pet the puppy on the shoulder or chest for 3 seconds and stop. Does puppy ask for more (nudge your hand)? Or do they walk away?

If puppy walks away, they have had enough and we need to respect our puppy's boundaries.

5 House Rule Myths

01 No People Food

Begging and stealing food is a concern most of us have. However, using "people" food won't create a monster. It's completely fine to give fresh foods as long as they are dog friendly.

02 No dogs on the furniture

This is a personal preference. Letting your puppy on the furniture won't create behaviour problems such as resource guarding. But your furniture might get licked on and scratched.

03 Go outside before your puppy

This comes from the dominance theory which has been debunked and is outdated! Puppy going out the door first isn't about dominance; it's just about excitement to go outside.

04 Puppy must be crate trained

A lot of puppies do not like the crate and crate training will need to be done gradually. Many pet parents don't have the time or patience for this. You don't need to crate train if it doesn't work for you.

05 Puppy needs to earn affection

This also comes from the outdated idea that everything must be earned. Imagine doing this to our spouse or children. It's completely unnecessary. Giving affection won't cause behaviour issues.

The Essentials

Flat collar and 6ft leash

Name tag and city registration

Stainless steel water bowl

Interactive feeders and toys

Training treats

Poo bags

Puppy shampoo and brush

Tooth brush and toothpaste

Nail clipper

Cleaning products

Dog bed, dog crate (optional)

Kong

Bones to chew

Harness

Variety of toys

Chapter One
Review

Picking A Puppy

- Look up breed(s) for information on grooming, character and energy
- Pick a suitable source for your puppy
- Ask lots of questions including:
    - Can you meet the parents?
    - Do they socialize they puppies?
    - Are there any health/behaviour issues in their lines?
    - What is the temperament of the puppy?
    - Where are the puppies held?

Car Safety

- Prepare for messes
- Use a crash proof harness
- Or use a crate or carrier

Puppy Proofing

- Hide wires
- Put plants higher up
- Clean up and put away knickknacks
- Hide garbages
- Put up gates/close doors to rooms
- Keep countertops clean and free from food

First Night

- Bed sharing is perfectly fine
- Crate or play pen to be in the same room
- Since most puppies have never slept alone before, being in a crate by themselves can be quite distressing.

NOTES

Chapter Two

This chapter focuses on socialization, and helps guide you to raise a happy, social and confident puppy.

Socialization
The best form of prevention.

Socialization often is put on the back burner of our "to-do" list because we feel a puppy with good manners is more important. However, socialization is the best form of prevention when it comes to fear, aggression, and unwanted behaviours like barking.

This period in their development is from 3-16 weeks old. This is when puppies are eager and willing to explore. This is why it is the top priority on your puppy training to-do list. To socialize our puppy is to create positive associations to a variety of new places and experiences, to help them feel safe and build new skills around distractions.

The American Veterinary Society of Animal Behaviour (AVSAB) urges puppy parents to begin socializing their puppy 1 week after their first round of vaccinations. Most breeders do the first round which means most puppies are ready to socialize as soon as they come home.

While there is a concern of disease and illness when socializing puppies, there are greater behavioural risks when we wait until a puppy is fully vaccinated. Many dogs are abandoned and euthanized due to behavioural issues; most of these issues are preventable with early socialization efforts.

Dog Body Language

Dogs express themselves with their body and vocalizations. They will communicate when they are happy, scared, stressed, or frustrated.

Most of the signs of stress are subtle and easily missed by us humans. This why some behaviours seem to "come out of nowhere".

Understanding dog body language is an acquired skill that takes lots of practice observing dogs. The key is to practice. The more we familiarize ourselves with the signs of stress, the more we actually see them!

COMMON SIGNS OF STRESS:

- Licking their nose
- Pulling their ears back
- Whale eye (seeing lots of the white)
- Panting
- Yawning
- Paw lift
- Avoiding eye contact
- Making self small
- Dandruff
- Hyper salivation
- Trembling
- Blinking eyes rapidly
- Suddenly sniffing the ground
- Losing focus on handler
- Refusing to take food

Next time you interact with your puppy, or when your puppy is playing with another dog, keep an eye out for these signs. When our puppy becomes stressed, we need to help relieve it. Here are a few things you can do:

- Remove them from the trigger
- Increase distance and guide puppy to walk away
- Use visual barriers

Note: comforting your puppy when they are afraid does not reinforce fear. It is absolutely fine to comfort your puppy and it won't make them more afraid next time. In fact, providing a safe space for them can make the experience less stressful and help your puppy be more open to exploring.

Creating Positive Experiences

Now that we know how to read our puppy's body language and figure out when they are uncomfortable, we are ready to start actively creating positive experiences during socialization.

To start creating positive experiences, we need to figure out what our puppy loves as a reward. Every puppy is different. Some love cheese, while others prefer some sort of meat as a reward. You may even have a puppy who will do anything for a good game of tug.

Exposing our puppy is not enough when it comes to socialization. Puppies are constantly making sense of their world. When we leave it to chance, we risk creating negative associations.

Once we have our puppy's favourite rewards (I suggest carrying a variety to keep things interesting), we will start checking experiences off our list. (See page 44 for the socialization checklist)

Here is an example:

You bring your puppy for a walk by a children's playground. You stop and puppy is watching the children run, play and scream.

You will start to use your food rewards liberally. Reward for:
- Looking at the children
- Looking away
- Looking at you
- Play a game of tug
- And practice some new skills

Then be off on your way. We want this experience to be fun for your puppy so they learn that:

children screaming = cheese

Let's say you go to the pet store. While there, guide our puppy to walk on the scale using cheese. Reward when:

They look at the scale They sniff the scale They put 1 paw up They stand on the scale

Again, we are creating an association:

scale = cheese

Puppy Play Skills

A big part of socializing your puppy is having them practice their play skills with other dogs. You will notice that each puppy has their own personality and play style.

Some puppies love to play "tag" where they chase and enjoy being chased. Others play more rough with a good wrestling match, and some like to bounce around and are a bit softer.

As humans, it's normal for us to feel stressed and overwhelmed when dogs growl, show their teeth and wrestle. These play styles, are just that, play! Play consists of practicing the following skills:

- Fighting
- Hunting
- Mating

Sequestering a puppy who plays a little rough won't teach them how to properly play and read other dogs. Puppies who play a little rough can be taught better play skills by:

1) Practicing their skills with a socialized, friendly adult dog
2) Learning new skills such as coming when called
3) Taking lots of breaks and performing consent tests (See next page about consent tests)

Signs of good play:
- **Change in roles**
    - Each puppy takes their turn chasing
    - Each puppy takes their turn being on top
- **Play signals**
    - Play face (kind of like a grin)
    - Play bow
    - Bouncy, exaggerated movements

- These act like winks, "it's just play!"
- **Self handicapping**
  - Larger dog lays down
  - They don't bite with full force
  - They don't body slam with full force

If we have a puppy who is shy or fearful, we will want to prioritize socialization and do it "gently". For instance, if our puppy seems afraid of other dogs:
- We introduce only 1 dog at a time. This makes it a lot less overwhelming. Ideally, we introduce a dog or puppy who is calmer.
- Use barriers like a baby gate where they have a visual but are not forced to interact.
- Encourage and reward looking at and investigating the other dogs.
- Perform lots of consent tests to ensure our puppy's comfort.

Now that we know a little more on how to spot good play and what to do if it isn't, we need to know how to choose a suitable playmate for our puppy. When choosing a playmate, we want to be mindful of the following:
- Age difference
- Size difference
- Play style

I would not feel comfortable letting a 3lbs puppy play with a 40lbs puppy. Although it is important for them to see each other and learn how to be around dogs of different sizes, I would carefully manage their interactions.

A puppy meeting many new dogs at the same time can be extremely overwhelming which is why I don't suggest dog parks for young puppies. It can be too much for your puppy to handle. (Dog parks also have a higher risk of disease and illness.)

Instead of a dog park, try these instead:
- Schedule play dates with 1 dog at a time
- Puppy socials
- Puppy group classes

Puppy socials and group puppy classes are great places to start socializing your puppy. Each instructor will have different exercises to practice which is fun if you decide to do more than 1 puppy class. This is a great opportunity for your puppy to practice their play skills with friends their age in a controlled setting. Any good puppy class will include play time, and know how to manage the puppies. The information from the previous page explains how to handle both types of puppies, so you know how to help your puppy have a good time playing.

When playing, we practice consent tests to ensure everyone is having fun.
We hold back the "bully", the one chasing, pinning or being rough with the other puppies. When held back, what does the "victim" do? (The puppy being chased or pinned)
- Do they come back for more? (This means it was play.)
- Or do they walk away? (This means they don't want to play anymore.)

The more often we practice consent tests, the better we get at spotting when play turns sour.

When to do a consent test:
- It's always the same puppy being chased or pinned down
- Play seems rough
- We're not sure everyone is having fun
- A lot of yelping
- Scuffles like nipping, snapping, barking, or a lot of growling.

If the "victim" puppy walks away, we will need to redirect or manage the "bully" so they don't continue bugging their friend who clearly said "no thank you". You can separate them, keep the puppies on leash, or engage the "bully" puppy to play with you or with a toy.

Building new skills while socializing

The next chapter covers a few new skills to teach your puppy. I do not include how to teach sit and down because most have already taught their puppy these skills. I focus on skills that are especially useful.

When practicing new skills, it's best to start in a calm environment such as your living room. This is to help set up an environment that promotes learning. It's much more difficult to learn something new when there are many other things going on at once. This is true for both humans and animals. Imagine studying for an exam while children are running around, the TV is loud and the dog is barking.

Once the puppy's new skills are reliable (they will perform the skill almost every time when asked), then you can start to practice them when you are out socializing your puppy.

Practicing skills while socializing is as important as the exposure itself. We want our puppy to learn that they can play and have fun, but also come when called and focus on us while friends are around.

The Checklist

SOUNDS

- [ ] Horns
- [ ] Sirens
- [ ] Fireworks
- [ ] Thunderstorm
- [ ] Oven Fan
- [ ] Vacuum

TEXTURES

- [ ] Grass
- [ ] Gravel
- [ ] Puddles
- [ ] Tile
- [ ] Wood
- [ ] Metal Grill
- [ ] Sand
- [ ] Snow

PEOPLE

- [ ] Women
- [ ] Men
- [ ] Teenagers
- [ ] Elderly
- [ ] Children
- [ ] People with Hats
- [ ] Delivery Person
- [ ] Wheelchair
- [ ] Joggers
- [ ] Cyclists

PLACES

- [ ] Playground
- [ ] Busy Street
- [ ] Pet Store
- [ ] Veterinary Clinic
- [ ] Elevator

ANIMALS

- [ ] Cats
- [ ] Big Dogs
- [ ] Small Dogs
- [ ] Birds
- [ ] Rabbits
- [ ] Horses
- [ ] Chickens
- [ ] Rats

BODY HANDLING

- [ ] Ears
- [ ] Tail
- [ ] Paws
- [ ] Mouth
- [ ] Being Hugged
- [ ] Nails
- [ ] Wearing Clothes

30-DAY
SOCIALIZATION CHALLENGE

01 Visit a pet store	02 Wear a hat and sunglasses	03 Introduce an umbrella	04 Play sounds of fireworks	05 Walk by a playground
06 Make a DIY obstacle course	07 Practice body handling	08 Find a puppy social	09 Play sounds of thunder	10 Go to a pet friendly store
11 Go to a drive thru	12 Walk in a puddle	13 Visit a busy city corner	14 Wear a big, winter jacket	15 Have puppy wear a shirt
16 Explore halloween decorations	17 Visit a park and watch joggers	18 Meet someone in a wheel chair	19 Walk by a playground	20 Visit a dog friend
21 Visit a skate park	22 Walk on gravel	23 Play in a ball pit	24 Play sounds of sirens	25 Car ride
26 Wear a mask/costume	27 Walk in the sand	28 Go on the scale at the vet or pet store	29 Practice wearing a cone	30 Make a DIY tunnel with a chair and blankets

Chapter Two
Review

Prioritize Socialization

- Socialization period is from 3-16 weeks of age
- Puppies are more willing to explore new things and meet new people
- Puppies are ready to socialize 1 week after their first round of vaccines
- Expose puppy to a variety of people, animals, places, textures and sounds

Dog Body Language

- Learn to spot signs of stress
- It's an acquired skill that takes practice
- Observe your puppy when they interact with people, animals and their environment
- Remove puppy from stressful situations
- It's okay to comfort your puppy when they are afraid

Positive experiences

- Help puppy feel safe when stressed
- Be proactive with socialization and help puppy create positive associations by using high value food rewards
- Happy talk and play are great to use in junction with food rewards
- Reward all good behaviours from puppy such as being curious, exploring, giving you etc contact...etc.

Puppy Play

- Find playmates of similar age, size and play style
- Avoid dog parks (overwhelming and risk of illness)
- Look for good play
    - Play signals
    - Change in roles
    - Self handicapping
- Perform consent tests often

NOTES

CHAPTER
THREE

The essential puppy life skills; this chapter will cover the important basics that will help you and your puppy navigate life together.

Ever heard the saying "can't teach an old dog new tricks"? Well, it's a myth! Dogs can learn new skills at any age! Yes, even senior dogs! While it can be easier to teach when they are younger, before certain habits set in, there is really no rush to teaching your puppy to sit, lie down or stay. They can learn these skills at any age!

As I mentioned in chapter 2, puppies are most eager and willing to explore between the ages of 3-16 weeks. This is why socialization will take priority during this time in your puppy's life.

This chapter will go over some key skills, their importance and how to use them while you socialize your puppy.

Training Concepts

Tips for success

- **Follow the plan:** Each skill is laid out, step by step. These plans are well vetted and have been practiced on hundreds of dogs. Use the checklists at the end of the chapter to track progress.

- **Do each step 10 times:** This is to ensure your puppy has had enough practice. Keep in mind that some pups require more practice, and that's okay! **If your pup is struggling:** If your puppy is having a hard time with a current step (they don't "get it" after 2 or 3 tries), go back a step.

- **Prepare your treats in advance**: Use a variety of food rewards and keep them close by. Cut up small pieces of cheese/hotdogs and keep a few ziplock bags in the freezer for future use.

- **Avoid punishment/corrections**: We don't always realize that we might tug on our dog's collar or say "no" when they get the answer wrong. The problem with punishment is it does not teach our dog the correct answer. If we follow our plan, adjust them as needed, there is no need for punishment or corrections.

• **Manage** puppy between training sessions to prevent unwanted behaviours from occurring (see page 69).

Why train using positive reinforcement?

There are different names for this type of training including: force free, humane or fear free training.

Essentially, we use rewards such as food to train new behaviours and create positive experiences. Management and creating good habits is used in lieu of corrections or punishment.

Fear, pain or intimidation such as popping their collar, rolling them on their side or using a harsh tone is unnecessary. The use of these methods can contribute to fear and anxiety which can lead to your puppy developing other unwanted behaviours.

Are life skills all about obedience?

Short answer is no. The skills learned in this chapter are used more often than traditional obedience behaviours.

Enjoy Being Touched
Body Handling Basics

An important skill to teach your puppy is how to enjoy being touched. Puppies are not born loving being touched and retrained. We are often surprised when our puppy acts defensively when they get groomed, or visit the vet.

Body handling is a big part of our daily life with our puppies. We touch them all the time to pet them, give them hugs, put on their harness or wipe their paws. We want them to feel comfortable with these types of interactions to help prevent fear and aggression.

Body handling is often put on the back burner when it comes to what we teach our new puppy. Teaching our puppy positive associations to being handled and restrained will help with:
• Grooming such as nail trims, baths and brushing
• Vet care such as general exams or treatments
• Putting on their harness/collar
• Wiping their paws
• Reduce puppy biting

We want to be proactive with body handling, which means we will practice these exercises using our pup's favourite food rewards, and take breaks when they seem uncomfortable. (See dog body language on page 37.)

Light handling and restraint

We will start with light handling to prepare your puppy for more "invasive" type handling such as being restrained, getting their nails trimmed and having their ears checked.

- Ears
- Mouth
- Eyes
- Paws
- Tail

Step 1: lightly touch puppy's ear for 1 second then give a treat.

Step 2: lightly touch puppy's ear for 3 seconds then give a treat.

Do step 1 and step 2 for each body part mentioned above. Next we will begin light restraints

Step 3: Hold puppy's ear for 3 seconds. You can try to flip it as if you are checking their ear. Then give a treat.

Do step 3 for each body part.

I encourage you to practice similar exercises for hugging, picking up your puppy, brushing their fur or clipping their nails. The goal is to create positive experiences to make these types of interactions easier for you and stress free for your puppy.

You Can Take My Toy
Resource Guarding Prevention

All dog behaviour has a genetic component and resource guarding is no exception. That does not mean that the behaviours cannot be modified or worked on. We will go through a few simple exercises to help teach your puppy that having their stuff taken away is nothing to worry about. Be sure to take your time for each exercise and repeat them weekly!

The Toy Switch

- Practice each step 10 times
- Prepare your puppy's favourite treats in advance and have them ready in a pouch or a jar

Step 1: Give your puppy a toy such as a rope toy, ball or plush. Take a step back and give puppy a few moments to get into their toy. Walk up to your puppy and place a few pieces of food next to them, then walk away.

Step 2: Repeat step 1 but this time take the toy away, give them a few pieces of food, and then give the toy back.

Food Bowl Bonuses

- Practice a few times a week
- Prepare your puppy's favourite treats in advance and have them ready in a pouch or jar
- Use a slow feeder bowl or kong

It's important to note that we will not bother our puppy while they eat. This exercise is to simply show our puppy that when they are eating, and we approach, good stuff happens. There is no reason to be uncomfortable with us near their food.

Give puppy their bowl of food and take a few steps back. While puppy is eating, take a few steps forward to approach and toss a few treats next to their bowl. Repeat 2-3 times or as many as you can during their feeding.

Coming When Called

is one of the most important skills you can teach your puppy. It can literally save their life. We do everything we can to manage our environment to prevent any sort of accidents. We keep our puppies on leash or use a long line when we want them to run and play. We make sure to keep gates closed and socialize them to new people and animals.

However, things will happen. A leash might break or get dropped. A gate or door might be left open. It's more common than we think (and it actually happened to me on several occasions). This is why coming when called is first on the list of skills to teach your new puppy.

Young puppies tend to stay close by which can be pretty deceiving. Before you know it, adolescence will begin and suddenly, our wonderfully "self trained" puppy begins to explore farther away and previously trained skills seemed to have "fallen out of their head".

It's best not to take your puppy's willingness to stay close for granted. Being proactive is so important.

Choosing your special word

When it comes to your puppy's recall cue, it's best to choose something different from "come" and "here". We often say these words, whether it is to our puppy or to someone else. We don't always follow this word with a reward, which will make it lose its value. After some time, the word "come" stops working.

Here are a few suggestions:
- Puppy puppy puppy
- Accio
- Chicken
- Cookie
- Boomerang
- Front

Once we have picked out our word, we will start creating a strong, positive association to this word. In order to do this, we need to have our puppy's favourite treats. I use anything stinky!

Here are a few ideas for high value rewards:
- Tripe (canned works well)
- Boiled chicken
- Sardines
- Cooked hamburger meat
- Old aged cheddar
- Pecorino Romano
- Salami

Any food reward should be cut into small, bite-sized pieces (about the size of your pinky nail).

Keep in mind, that what is high value for one dog, is different for another dog. I suggest auditioning different types of treats and keep a variety of them on hand.

Be prepared
- Have a treat pouch each time you train and whenever you go out with puppy.
- Prepare your puppy's favourite treats in advance.
- Cut up bite-sized pieces, place them individual bags and store them in the freezer.

Exercise #1: Intro to the cue

Distractions: None.

To begin, have your food rewards prepared in advance. While your puppy is hanging out in the same room as you, suddenly call them using your special word.

Encourage puppy to come up to you. Use "kissy" sounds, tap on your thighs or take a few quick steps backwards.

When puppy approaches, reward with 2-3 small pieces of food.

Repeat 10 times.

Exercise #2: Out of view

Distractions: Be in different rooms.

Prepare treats in advance.

Your puppy is in another room, with no other distraction. Call your puppy using your special word.

Encourage puppy to come to you by using kissy sounds and tapping on your thighs.

Reward with 2-3 pieces of food.

Repeat 10 times.

If puppy has a tough time coming when they are in another room, go back to the first exercise for a few repetitions. Then try again.

Leash Skills

Bubble exercises are fun and super helpful to practice with your puppy. They help with leash skills and building focus with your puppy.

We're going to go over a few "bubble" exercises. I call them bubble exercises because we are going to teach your puppy that your bubble is the best place to be. The more value we put into our bubble, the more our puppy will want to be there.

Exercise: Staying Close

You'll need:
• Variety of treats
• Open space like your living room or yard

Have a handful of treats in your hand and hold it high on your belly. Walk around and reward each time your puppy looks at you and each time they follow. Suddenly change direction, change your pace to make it more fun and challenging.

Your puppy has to come close to get the treat, which will encourage and reward proximity!

Exercise: Touch!

Step 1: You will have your hand open as if you are showing the number 4. Under your thumb, will be a treat hiding.

Hold out your hand out to your puppy, they will come sniff out the treat. When they do, say "yes" and give them the treat.

Repeat 10 times.

Step 2: Hold your hand out, showing the number 4 without a treat under your thumb. When puppy comes to sniff your hand, say "yes" and reward. Repeat 10 times.

Step 3: Now, same as step 2 but say the word "touch" when you present your hand. Repeat 10 times.

Exercise: Middle

This is especially fun to teach, and very useful. I've used it while waiting in line at the pet store, while waiting at a cross walk or as a way to keep my puppy close.

Step 1: Guide your puppy to stand between your legs with a treat. Reward them in this position. Then, toss a treat away and do it again.

Step2: Pretend to have a treat in your hand, then guide your puppy between your legs then reward them in position.

Step 3: We are now going to introduce the cue "middle". Say "middle", then guide your puppy between your legs. Reward in position.

Repeat each step 10 times.

Stay On A Mat

Stay on a mat is probably the most used skill in my house. I use it when we cook and eat dinner, when guests arrive and when our baby arrived. The mat gives your puppy a specific spot to go to, which makes it less confusing and sets your puppy up for success!

Step 1: Guide your puppy onto a mat and guide them into a down. Sit in front of them and feed them a treat every 2-3 seconds for 15-30 seconds, then ask them to get off and toss a treat. Repeat 10 times.

Step 2: Have your puppy lay on their mat. You take one step to the side, come back and give a reward. Repeat 10 times only doing 1 step.

Step 3: Take 2 steps to the side, come back and reward. Repeat 10 times.

Step 4: You will repeat step 3 for 3 steps, then 4 steps...etc. Until you are eventually able to walk around your puppy while they lay on their mat.

Leave It

I love to teach leave it. It's a skill that is so versatile and used for so much more then you would think.

I use it to stop puppy from grabbing an "illegal" item, when I want my dog to move away from something, for counter surfing, and even leash reactivity.

Let's go over the basics of leave it:

Step 1: Place a few pieces of food in your hand. Close your hand into a fist then present it to your puppy. Let them lick and sniff your hand. **Don't pull your hand away.** Just wait.

At the split second that your puppy stops sniffing/licking/nibbling your hand, say "yes", then reward.

Repeat until your puppy no longer tries to mug you on the first try.

Step 2: This step can be hard for a lot of puppies, so go back to step 1 as needed.

Hold a treat out (your hand is open) for 1 second, about 1-2 feet away from your puppy. Pull your hand away if they come to sniff/take the treat early.

Reward when puppy stays put, or hesitates.

Step 3: Repeat step 2, but hold the treat out for 3 seconds.

Pull hand away if puppy tries to sniff/take the treat early.

Reward when puppy stays put, or hesitates.

Step 4: Introduce the cue "leave it". Say "leave it", then present a treat in your hand, hold it out for 3 seconds. Then reward puppy.

Step 5: Place a piece of food on the floor for 1 second and say "leave it". Put your hand over the food if puppy tries to take it. Reward when they stay put.

Training Plans

- Do each step 10 times.
- After 2-3 mistakes, go back a step.

Coming When Called

Step 1: Using your special word, call your puppy while in the same room. Reward with 2-3 pieces of high value treats.

Step 2: Call your puppy from another room. Reward with 2-3 pieces of high value treats.

Stay Close

Walk around and reward each time your puppy looks at you and each time they take a step to follow.

Touch!

Step 1: With a treat under your thumb, hold your hand out to your puppy. Reward when they put their nose to your hand.

Step 2: Pretend to have a treat under your thumb. Hold your hand out to your puppy. Reward when they put their nose to your hand.

Step 3: Say "touch" then present your hand. Reward when puppy puts their nose to your hand.

Middle

Step 1: Guide your puppy to stand between your legs with a treat. Reward them in this position.

Step 2: Pretend to have a treat in your hand, then guide your puppy between your legs then reward them in position.

Step 3: Say "middle", then guide your puppy between your legs. Reward in position.

Stay on a mat

Step 1: Guide your puppy onto a mat and guide them into a down. Sit in front of them and feed them a treat every 2-3 seconds for 15-30 seconds.

Step 2: Have your puppy lay on their mat. You take one step to the side, come back and give a reward.

Step 3: Take 2 steps to the side, come back and reward.

Step 4: You will repeat step 3 for 3 steps, then 4 steps...etc.

Leave it

Step 1: Hold a fist full of treats out 1-2 ft away from your puppy. Let them sniff, lick, nibble your hand. When they stop, even for a split second, reward!

Step 2: Hold a treat out (your hand is open) for 1 second, about 1-2 feet away from your puppy. Reward when your puppy hesitates or stays put.

Step 3: Repeat step 2, but hold the treat out for 3 seconds. Reward when your puppy hesitates or stays put.

Step 4: Say "leave it", then present a treat in your hand, hold it out for 3 seconds. Then reward puppy.

Step 5: Place a piece of food on the floor for 1 second and say "leave it" then give puppy the treat.

NOTES

CHAPTER FOUR

Create Good Habits Early

Prevent unwanted behaviours with a proactive approach.

What's Normal Puppy Behaviour?

Creating good habits early is one of the keys (alongside socialization) to preventing a laundry list of unwanted behaviours. Most unwanted behaviours are in fact normal.

- Digging
- Chewing
- Barking
- Foraging for food
- Chasing

Keep in mind that these types of behaviours don't always need to be "fixed". They are not a problem to our dogs, but can be unpleasant or annoying when the time or target is not appropriate. Our dogs (and puppies!) have basic needs that must be met. They need more than just food, water and shelter. Providing enrichment and legal outlets for their natural, instinctive behaviours is an important part of their mental well being.

Suppressing these behaviours can have the opposite effect. The need is always there and if it's not being met, it will manifest itself in other ways. This is often where unwanted behaviours come from. For example: if we do not provide mental enrichment such as foraging for food through puzzles, kongs and games, your dog is more likely to seek out food in your kitchen, outside on walks and in garbages.

In this chapter, we will help you understand what is normal in your puppy, give you ideas for outlets and enrichment, and show you how to use the training exercises from the previous chapter to help your puppy create good habits.

Managing Your Puppy

The first thing we need to do is manage both your puppy and the environment to prevent your puppy from "getting into trouble". I put quotations because unwanted behaviours are only a problem to us. Our puppies love to chew. Think of it as a favourite pastime like reading a book or watching your favourite TV show.

Puppy proofing your home is the best way to start (see page 19). By removing access to certain spaces such as bedrooms and bathrooms, we are reducing the probability that our puppy will get into something.

Management is not forever. We use it until we have full confidence that our puppy has learned what is theirs to chew, that they are housetrained and that we helped teach them good habits. There is no specific age when this happens. For some we can take down the gates around 8-9 months old, while for others it's after 2 years old. You know your puppy best.

I can give you a piece of advice, something I learned the hard way, is not to rush this stage. Don't remove management too early because it's not nice to look at or a little inconvenient.

I promise, it's worth leaving the gates up just a little longer. There are a few general management strategies that you can easily implement to make life a little easier with your puppy:
• Using baby gates
• Closing doors to certain rooms
• Keeping puppy on leash
• Having a puppy proofed space when they cannot be supervised
• Using a crate or pen

You may even decide to set up a few management strategies and that is an excellent idea!

Remember, it's not for forever. This is the first part of creating good habits. We are also going to provide enrichment and training. It's all about setting our puppy up for success!

Should you use the crate?

There is no clear, right answer. Is crate training a good idea? Of course. There may come a time where your puppy might need to be crated for recovery after a surgery or travel. However, for most puppies and dogs, being in a crate is quite distressing. There are many ways to manage our puppy without the use of a crate.

If your puppy shows signs of distress, I would suggest using a different form of management.

Either way, your puppy will need to be gradually introduced to the crate. (See crate training on page 110).

Enrichment

There are so many ways to provide enrichment to our dogs. The most popular are food puzzles. This is one of the easiest ways to incorporate enrichment into your puppy's daily life. We use a portion of their meal and ask them to work for it. Using their meal as enrichment can help keep your puppy busy for longer. It's important to note that your puppy does not need to work for every piece of food they get.

Food enrichment can include:
- Stuffed kongs
- Puzzle feeders
- Scatter feeding (throwing their food in the grass)
- Sniffing mats
- Lickimats
- Training

Dogs are foragers and are often on the look out for food. If we don't provide them with legal outlets for this natural instinct, they will put it to use by counter surfing, going through the garbage and picking up food they find outside on walks.

Enrichment for unwanted behaviours

Let's look at a few behaviours that we can curb by offering it with enrichment:

Digging:

Most dogs love to dig! Lagotto Romagnolo's were bred for it! Dogs dig for all sorts of reasons like to find a cool spot to lay in, to hide a treasure, or to find a treasure!

For those who live in dog-friendly areas, a beach with sand can be a perfect place to encourage digging. If you live somewhere less accommodating to dogs, you may consider building your own sand box for your dog.

A children's pool with sand, or a children's sand box are perfect examples of making a DIY digging pit. Hide your puppy's favourite toy, bones and treats to encourage them to dig.

When puppy is outside, they need to be closely supervised so you can redirect them to their sand box should they try to dig in your flower box.

Chewing:

Like reading a book is for us, chewing is a popular pastime for dogs. It may come as a surprise to learn that chewing is not a phase that goes away with age. While some dogs show less interest for it as they age, most continue to love gnawing on a hearty bone or a stick.

We don't want puppy chewing on our shoes or furniture, therefore we will need to provide suitable chewing options. Here are a few favourites in our home:

- Bully sticks
- Chicken feet
- Himalayan yak chews
- Split deer antlers

Keep in mind that every puppy is different. You might end up buying a few different kinds to see which your puppy enjoys. If you are unsure about allergies, or stomach upset, it's best to chat with your veterinary team.

How much exercise can I give my puppy?

The general rule of thumb is their age in months x 5 minutes

2 months old = 10 minutes

3 months old = 15 minutes

4 months old = 20 minutes

Chasing:

Chasing has a strong genetic component. Dogs bred for hunting and herding will chase small critters, moving objects like cars and even children! There are a few ways to meet their needs and practice this behaviour when it's appropriate and of course management will be needed.

- Flirt pole (stuffed animal on a long line - like a cat toy but for dogs)
- Lure coursing
- Fetch

With young puppies, we want to make sure we don't over do it on the physical exercise and repetitive movements, as they are still growing.

Sniffing:

Scent dogs have a particular drive for sniffing, but in general, all dogs enjoy it. A dog's nose has 300 million smell receptors where a human has only 6 million. This is an incredible super power in our dogs!

There are a few ways to encourage sniffing:
- Sniffing during walks (I let my dogs sniff as long as they want)
- Sniffing mats (to sniff out food!)
- Nosework classes
- Hide and seek
- Hide food around the house (or yard)

Sniffing on walks is one of the best (and easiest) ways to incorporate enrichment into our puppy's daily life. It allows them to explore and learn about their world and use that beautiful nose to its full potential. There are no rules for sniffing. We might be tempted to hurry our dog along to get a long walk in, but our dog's nose is working at full capacity; by really getting that brain working, and puppy is burning mental energy.

Next time you walk your puppy, let them set the pace, sniff as long as they want, and even choose the route. You might be surprised about where you end up!

1-2-3
Preventing Unwanted Behaviours

STEP 1

Management by preventing the behaviour from occurring

STEP 2

Provide **legal outlets** for your puppy's instinctive behaviours

STEP 3

Teach **new skills** to give puppy more information on what is okay

Teaching New Skills

In chapter 3, we covered the basic training of important life skills. In this next section, we will look at how we can incorporate these skills into daily life with our puppy.

Remember, it will be important to continue managing puppy's environment to prevent rehearsing unwanted behaviours.

Prepping and eating dinner
(And prevent counter surfing)
Management: use gates/crate to prevent access to the kitchen, or keep puppy on leash.

Training:
Stay on a mat and leave it are very useful in the kitchen. Once we began the basics of these skills, we can practice them in the kitchen.
- Place a mat in or next to the kitchen and ask your puppy to lay down.
- Reward puppy every 5-10 seconds for staying. (or reward 3-5 seconds if they are having a tough time)

We are teaching puppy that the way to get food is to stay away from the food!

Use a bully stick or stuffed kong while rewarding puppy for staying on their mat. The more we practice and make a habit out of this, the easier it is for our puppy to learn.

With leave it, we will repeat the same exercises from page 46, but now incorporate different foods. You can use dog friendly meats and vegetables.

For example, instead of putting a piece of kibble or dried treat on the ground, you can put a piece of carrot or turkey. The more we practice with everyday foods, our puppy will begin to generalize that "leave it" is for all foods.

Greeting guests
Management: Put puppy behind a gate or keep them on leash until training has progressed.

Training:
Sit stay: similar to stay on a mat, we can train our puppy to sit to greet guests. This strategy can also be used for greeting people when

you are out on a walk. Note: your puppy does not need to say hi to everyone they meet on walks.

Step 1: With someone who is already home, have them exit, knock, and then come in. Guide puppy into a sit and feed a few treats while they stay in that position.

Step 2: Repeat step 1 with someone who is after returning home from work.

Step 3: Practice with deliveries and guests.

Taking "illegal" items

Illegal items are anything that our puppy should not take to chew or play with such as socks, slippers, underwear or tissue paper. Management: Keep doors to certain rooms closed, use gates to block access and keep puppy on leash.

• Trade the item for a piece of high value food! Don't chase.
• Consider tossing the treat away so you have time to take the "illegal" item when they go get the treat.

Training:

Leave it will be your go-to for illegal items. It will be important to practice with a few select items such as:

• Socks
• Tissue paper

Repeat steps 2-5 of the leave it plan (page 46) with these items. Start with something easy like a clean paper towel, then a dirty one.

For example:

Hold out a paper towel for 3 seconds. If puppy tries to take it, remove your hand quickly and try again. When puppy stays put, reward with a treat.

It's important to note if your puppy grabs an item and begins to "guard" it by:
- Growling
- Snapping
- Hovering over the item
- Running away with it

This is a red flag and requires intervention.

If this happens, do the following:
- Back away
- Grab a handful of treats and toss them away so puppy leaves the object
- If treats don't work, go get their leash/collar like you're going for a walk
- And if they still don't leave the object, try ringing the door bell

It's important not to punish your puppy when they resource guard. First, it may remove their warning signal (the growl or when they show their teeth), and can increase intensity of their reaction by biting.

Look at the exercises on resource guarding prevention on page 41. If you are struggling, reach out to a certified professional, such as myself, to help guide you.

A professional will help you set up proper management to avoid triggering your puppy, give you a concrete plan, and help guide you each step of the way.

Chapter Four
Review

Normal Dog Behaviours

Normal dog behaviours are not a problem for our dogs but can be annoying to us.

Provide **legal outlets** through exercise and enrichment, **manage** puppy to prevent them from going it and **teach new skills.**

Management & Enrichment

- Prevent puppy from rehearsing unwanted behaviours by managing their environment
- Provide daily enrichment through food puzzles, training and sniffing

Counter Surfing

- Manage when not training. Do not leave food accessible. Use gates or keep puppy on a leash
- Practice "Stay on a Mat" for meal prep and eating dinner
- Practice "Leave It" for different types of dog friendly foods

Greetings

- Manage by using gates or keep puppy on a leash when people arrive
- Practice a "Sit Stay":
  - People in your home pretending to arrive
  - People in your home arriving from work
  - Guests and delivery people

Illegal Items

- Manage by:
    - Close doors to certain rooms such as bedrooms and the bathroom
    - Tidy up
- Practice "Leave It" for a variety of "illegal" items
- Practice resource guarding prevention exercises (page XX)

If puppy resource guards: growls, shows teeth, hides or hovers over item:

- Back away
- Toss treats away
- Grab their leash to "go for a walk"
- Ring the door bell
- Call a certified professional to help

NOTES

CHAPTER
FIVE

Puppy Biting 101

Puppy Biting 101

With the fuzzy puppy fur and sweet puppy breath comes the sharp little daggers we call puppy teeth. After raising my own puppies, and working with hundreds of puppy clients, trust me when I say, I truly understand how unpleasant puppy biting is.

Dogs explore the world with their mouth. They use it for the obvious, play and grooming, but also to pick up sticks, even to taste a smell! Young puppies have not had enough practice to hone their skills yet.

In this chapter, we will talk about what is normal puppy biting, how to teach your puppy to control their strength, how to reduce and redirect the biting.

What's normal biting?

This may seem like an odd topic, but it's important to clarify that not all biting is the same. Like a dog of any age, puppies can bite when they are afraid. It's important to distinguish between play and fear.

For example: if your puppy bites you each time you try to pet them, it is possible your puppy is uncomfortable with being touched. Remember in Chapter 3 when I said, "puppies are not born loving being touched and restrained?" Therefore, it's entirely possible that the bite is from fear.

Another example: If you are playing with your puppy and then they growl and bite you, you might think this biting is aggressive. But looking back at puppy play in chapter 2, we know that growling and biting is how puppies play.

The first type of biting is not normal and requires intervention through management and training. (See body handling exercises on page 40)

If you are unsure if puppy is uncomfortable, check out page 27 on dog body language.

Fearful Biting

If you suspect fear in your puppy, there are a few things we can do to help them feel more comfortable.

First is management. (Are you even surprised? Ha!) We want our puppy to be happy and comfortable, therefore we will need to reduce their exposure to potential triggers.

If puppy does not seem comfortable with being touched, we will advocate for them by telling people not to touch the puppy, and finding a veterinarian and groomer who uses Fear Free techniques.

If puppy is uncomfortable when we approach them while they are eating or playing with a toy, we will have them eat in their crate or behind a gate.

It's important that we do not force puppy when they are afraid. This will only increase their stress and anxiety. In the long term, your puppy's fear can get worse and their triggers may even grow.

Extreme fear or shyness in young puppies is a red flag. It does not necessarily mean that your puppy experienced abuse but probably lacked early socialization or was born from a mother who was stressed during pregnancy or experienced fear herself.

I suggest writing down your puppy's potential triggers. For example:
• Children
• Strangers
• Being approached while eating
• Other dogs
• Specific sounds...etc

Once you start this list, we can begin proactively creating positive associations (page 38) to each of these triggers.

We can achieve this by presenting the trigger at a low level. This can mean, we are at a distance, there is a visual barrier, starting with smells, or playing sounds on a low volume.

How to find a certified professional:

The professional uses humane, fear free techniques.
They are certified by:

- Academy For Dog Trainers
- Karen Pryor Academy
- Fear Free Certified
- Pet Professional Accreditation
- Certified Separation Anxiety Trainer

From there, we will use our puppies favourite treats; whenever these triggers are present, we will lavish our puppy with cheese and happy talk. Keep it short and sweet.

If you feel like you are in way over your head in dealing with your puppy's fears, I strongly suggest working with a certified professional!

Playful Biting

Playful biting by puppies is completely normal and to be expected. Before we teach them not to bite, we must teach them to control how hard they bite. This is called acquired bite inhibition (ABI).

There is not much evidence that ABI can be taught to older dogs. It seems to be much easier when puppies are young.

They learn ABI mostly from playing with their litter and mother. When a puppy's bite is too hard, the other will yelp and offer some signs of stress as a way to cool down the play. You might even see dogs "correcting" each other with growls and snaps.

Keep in mind, that dogs do this to one another. Humans should not. It is not recommend to growl, pin down or physically correct your puppy. This is because these methods require fear, pain and intimidation which is not necessary when teaching animals. (Imagine growling at a lion...)

There are a few ways to work on your puppy's ABI:
- Letting low level play biting happen.These don't hurt or hurt very little and don't cause bruises or cuts.
- When puppy bites too hard, stop play (pause) and move to another area (like behind a gate) if puppy continues to bite. Like a time out, but very briefly, just a few seconds.
- Redirect puppy when bites are too hard. Take out their favourite toy and make it come alive through a fun game of tug.

Once puppy's bites seem to be soft most of the time, then we can start to work on not biting at all. We teach ABI because it'll help your puppy control their strength as they get older. They may continue to play bite as they mature, or if they bite from being scared or hurt, the strength is likely to be a lot softer.

How to reduce puppy biting:

Enrichment toys:
One of the best ways to keep your puppy's mouth occupied, is by giving them bones to chew and puzzle feeders to work on. This provides them with an outlet to their biting. Remember, dogs love to chew! (See page 70 for more ideas.)

Variety of toys:
Make sure puppy has a variety of toys, which can help keep their mouth busy and ease their teething. There are so many different kinds of toys that you will need to try a few to see what your pup loves the most. I keep a few toys on rotation to keep things interesting.

Rope toys, plush toys, nylon bones and anything that squeaks is a hit in our house.

Appropriate chews:
While this was mentioned in the enrichment section, I feel it deserves its own section. Providing bones to chew will be one of best ways to save you from puppy's biting. There are so many different types, that again, you will need to try a few to see what your puppy enjoys the most.

Here are just a few examples:
- Bully sticks
- Yak chews
- Chicken feet
- Tracheas
- No hide bones
- Sweet potatoes
- Dental sticks

Physical exercise:
How much exercise your pup needs will depend on their age, breed and individual character. Some breeds require a lot more physical exercise then others. The rule of thumb is 5 minutes per month of age. While we want to avoid too much repetitive movement while they are growing, playing tug, fetch, walking and running are great ways to burn your pups' energy.

If ever you are not sure about what is appropriate for your puppy, reach out to your veterinary team.

Nap time:
Puppies need a lot of sleep and they can sleep up to 18-20 hours a day! Like with children, when they are over tired, they get silly. Do you ever notice that at certain times a day, your puppy's biting is relentless? If you exhausted all other efforts (enrichment, bones, play, exercise and toys), then it might be time for a nap.

- Give them a bone or kong to chew in their puppy-proofed space
- Snuggle on the couch
- Provide a bed close by to you

New skills:

A few skills we worked on in chapter 3 can help curb your puppy's biting. This is done by creating new association around your hands. Here are few things you can teach:
- Leave it
- Touch
- Body handling exercises
- Fetch a toy
- Drop it

With these skills, they will learn different ways to interact with us and our hands without biting.

Socialization:

Playing with other puppies is a great way for your pup to practice their ABI. The more practice they get, the better they will be at controlling their mouth. Other puppies and friendly dogs can be great teachers! (See page 40 for puppy play.)

Playing With Your Puppy

Playing with your puppy is super beneficial. It will help you bond together, learn more about your puppy, their interests, and teach your puppy how to appropriately interact with you. It's a great way to get them to practice their new skills!

Some people feel uncomfortable with how your puppy plays because the puppy bites, growls or barks. Know that this type of play is completely normal, but feelings of discomfort toward dog play is still valid. It's okay if you feel uncomfortable. There are different ways to play with your puppy and we will go through each of them. As you practice playing together, you will start to feel more comfortable!

Find the treats!
Have your pup sit or be held on leash. Place treats around the room in easy to spot places (corners, by their bed...etc). Then release them by saying, "Go find it"!

This is a fun game to get your puppy to use their nose (very enriching!), practice waiting and explore their space.

As puppy gets better at finding the treats, you can hide them in more challenging spots.

Fetch!
Hunting and working breeds love fetch! Some other dogs are not too into it which is fine! It might be a fun game to try to see if it piques your puppy's interest.

Here's how to start:
Throw their favourite toy, not too far. When puppy picks up the item say "yes" and offer a treat. You can eventually say "yes" when puppy

is running back with the toy. Later, you can wait to say "yes" until they bring the toy all the way back to you.

For dogs who seem to only like it when you throw, but not take their toy, have a second toy to throw when they come back.

Trick training
This is especially fun and a great way for older children to interact with the puppy. Tricks like give the paw, middle, spin, play dead, sit pretty, etc. are easy to teach.

It also creates a fun way for you pup to interact with your without using their teeth!

Flirt pole:
I briefly mentioned this in the enrichment section of chapter 4. A flirt pole is a stuffed toy (usually resembling a small animal) on a string and a stick (kind of like a cat toy.)

Some dogs love to chase and this is a great way to encourage their instinctive behaviours in a way that is fun for both us and them!

You can easily make a DIY flirt pole with a plush toy, rope and a broom stick.

Slowly drag the stuffed animal and make sudden movements to get the chase going. Let your dog catch it and work on "drop it" to have them let go.

Tug:
This game is a lot of fun! It helps burn their energy and we can even work on basic skills while playing!

There is a misconception that tug will make your puppy aggressive. There is no evidence that this is true, and tug is a great game to play with your puppy!

We will want to work on "drop it" and "take it" while playing, which will help start and stop the game.

Here's how to train "drop it":

Step 1: Start to play tug with your puppy. When they have hold of the toy, stop moving and hold a treat out from your other hand. When puppy let's go of the toy, say "yes", reward with a treat. Repeat 10 times.

Step 2: Repeat step 1 but pretend to hold out a treat. When puppy lets go, say "yes", and reward with a treat. Repeat 10 times.

Step 3: While playing tug, stop moving, say "drop it", then hold out your hand. When puppy lets go, give a treat. Repeat 10 times.

When playing tug, it's good to practice stopping play. You can stop it with "drop it", ask puppy to sit and then say "take it" and encourage them to continue playing. This is a great way to practice impulse control when they are amped up!

If puppy starts to bite you during tug:
The first rule of tug is: teeth on toy only. Sometimes their mouth slips but dogs with experience have excellent mouth awareness and can control the position of their bite.

If puppy bites, encourage them to grab the toy. If they continue to bite you, take a break. Give them a chew, and give them some time to settle down.

It's normal for puppies to bite. They need practice controlling their strength and perfecting their accuracy. The more we play with our puppy, the better they will get. When playing tug, remember to:
• Practice drop it to let go of toy
• Work in basic skills like sit
• Use a cue like "take it" to let them know that the game is back on

Growling and showing teeth during tug is normal. It's just play! If this type of play makes you uncomfortable, you can start with less intense types of play. But your puppy should get some time to play tug to practice their skills.

Puppy biting conclusion:

Biting and chewing are a normal part of how puppies interact with their world. With time and practice, puppies will learn how to control their strength, their accuracy when biting and learn what type of play is appropriate with us.

To work on reducing puppy biting, we need to:
• Teach ABI (aquired bite inhibition)
• Let them play with other puppies
• Provide enrichment toys
• Provide a variety of chew toys
• Give them enough physical exercise
• Give them enough nap time or down time
• Practice playing with our puppy

NOTES

CHAPTER
Six

HOUSETRAINING

House Training 101

Most puppies do not come home being house trained. Some breeders are proactive and start their puppies with pee pads or teach them to use litter boxes.

Some puppies also seem to house train themselves quite easily. People who acquire those puppies should count their lucky stars because they are few and far between. In general, house training a puppy can be a bit of a process. There are a lot of misconceptions. So let's start there:

House training myths:

#1 You need to punish your puppy for messing in the house
This is totally false. It may seem counterintuitive to not punish our puppies for peeing inside. But often this "punishment" is done with force, loud voices, or other aversive measures. We want to avoid such punishment for a few reasons. Punishing your puppy for peeing inside can:

- Scare your puppy and create a negative association to you.
- Teach your puppy to hide when they pee. (under beds or behind the couch)
- Puppy can learn that peeing in front of you is dangerous. Thus they won't go while out on a walk and wait to go behind the couch when they get home

#2 Don't clean it in front of them
While this isn't detrimental to your puppy's wellbeing because it's not punishment. But it's just silly. Simply clean up the mess with an odour deodorizer.

#3 You need a crate to house train
Using a crate can definitely be helpful, but it's not the only way to

manage our puppy to reduce messes. Many puppies don't like the crate and it can be distressing!

#4 Rubbing their nose in it will help them learn not to pee inside
Just like myth 1, rubbing their nose in their pee is definitely not pleasant and can create negative associations to you, to peeing in front of you and to being handled. Do not do this to your puppy.

Appropriate Potty Area

When puppy first comes home, it's a good idea to determine where the appropriate potty area will be. There are a few great options to choose from!

Outside potty
It is perfectly acceptable to simply let your puppy out in the yard to let them potty. If this is what works best for you, then that's perfectly okay! We can actually be more proactive and train our puppy to use a specific outdoor spot.
- Specific spot in your yard
    - You can use stones, mulch, grass or sand
- Specific spot at the beginning of your walk
- Or a balcony potty

Balcony Potty
Balcony potties can be especially useful if you live in an apartment or condo, where it may be difficult to take puppy out in a prompt manner.

There are a few ways to create a balcony potty:
- Grass pad or box.
    - You can use real grass or fake grass that you can hose down.
- Box with mulch, or wood type "litter".

Indoor Potty

There are a few reasons you might need an indoor potty.

- You live in an apartment or condo
- You or puppy has a medical condition
- You have a fearful puppy
- Puppy will be alone for longer than they can hold it

It's a good idea to have an indoor potty planned out in case your puppy is fearful or if left alone for a longer period of time.

Here are a few examples of an indoor potty:

- Fake grass pad
- Reusable potty pad
- Disposable potty pad
- Litter box with wood chips

If you got your puppy from a reputable breeder or rescue, they probably started the house training process with the puppies. I suggest inquiring to see what they used so we can be consistent. This will help puppy in your house training efforts.

The Extra Potty Details

Potty cues

All dogs will give a sign that says "I need to potty", whether it was intended to communicate with us or not. We will observe our puppy so we can learn what their specific potty signs are. Not all dogs are the same, so take some time observing your puppy to learn their cues.

Some examples of these cutes are:
- Suddenly sniffing the ground
- Walking in a circle
- Squatting
- Scratching the ground or the door
- Beginning to be restless
- Suddenly barking

We can also teach a potty cue like ringing a door bell. This can be useful if your puppy is hard to read or if their cue is bothersome (for example if they scratch or bark at the door.)

Ring a door bell
First, you will want to teach the cue "touch" (see page 44). Then we can introduce the touch cue to a door bell. You can buy a potty bell online or make one yourself with ribbon and a bell.

You will want to practice teaching your puppy to touch the bell before trying to get them to use it to potty.

Step 1: Hold out the bell and ask puppy to touch it. Reward when they do. If puppy seems fearful or unsure, take your time with this step. You can make it easier by asking your puppy to touch your hand while you hold the bell.

Step 2: Once puppy happily touches the bell, we can start associating it to potty times.

Ask puppy to ring the bell to go outside when you are sure they have to potty:
- First thing in the morning
- After meals
- After playing
- After a nap
- After they display other potty cues

House training red flags

There are a few red flags we need to be aware of when it comes to our puppy's health. The following signs may require medical intervention and you should call your veterinarian to discuss what you should do next:

- Urine with a strong odour
- Excessive urinating
- Excessive licking genitals
- Signs of painful or difficult urination
- Blood in urine
- Diarrhea
- Constipation
- Black, tarry feces
- Lapses in housetraining in a previously house trained dog

Handling Messes

We began this chapter with some myth busting. You have an idea of what not to do: don't scold puppy, don't scare them and don't rub their noses in it. Now, what should you do if your puppy makes a mess in the house?

The most important thing to do is a thorough clean up to remove waste and odours. If puppy urinated on a bed, cushion or carpet, we will need to deodorize it as best we can.

Here is a great recipe I use:
- 1 part vinegar
- 2 parts water
- A few drops of dish soap

You can also try to get a heavy duty cleaner to deep clean a carpet or couch. We want to make sure it's properly cleaned. After cleaning, we will need to manage our puppy better to prevent accidents next time. We will go over this more on the next page.

If puppy is in the middle of peeing:
There are 2 things we can do. We can hustle puppy outside but a word of caution, if you are quick to react, you might scare your puppy. Therefore, if you can bring them outside, do so gently.

The other option is to simply let them finish. We missed our chance to bring them to their spot. We will need to keep an eye out for those potty cues, continue working on the bell and manage our puppy better.

Why don't we punish them when they potty inside?
Unfortunately, there isn't a clear way to communicate to our puppy that this inside spot is not okay that does not include some sort of fear tactic. It's best to be proactive with management and training instead! Remember we want to avoid creating negative associations.

House Training 1-2-3

Now that we have our puppy's potty area sorted, we are ready for the next steps in house training.

Step 1: Management
The first thing we need to do is manage their space closely. If puppy has too much room to wander freely, we can be almost certain that accidents will happen.
• Here are a few management strategies to put in place:
• Set up gates and close doors
• Use a puppy-proofed room, play pen or crate when unsupervised
• Keep puppy on your lap or on leash to keep them close to you

If puppy will be alone for longer then they can hold it, we will need to provide an appropriate indoor potty area. This will help protect your house training efforts. (See page 69 for examples.) Remember that management is not forever. The better we can manage our puppy now, the quicker we can get them house trained!

Step 2: Reward

Once management is set up, we will encourage our puppy to go to their potty area. We will go there often, and reward each time they pee or poo. Relieving themselves is "self rewarding", because it's a relief from needing to pee. Giving a food reward is an added bonus!

Bring puppy to their potty area:
- When they wake up
- After eating or drinking
- During and after playing
- When you notice potty cues

What if puppy doesn't "go"?
1. Bring puppy to their spot and wait 5 minutes.
2. If no elimination occurs, bring them back inside for 10-15 minutes and tightly manage.
3. Go back outside for 5 minutes and reward when they eliminate. If they don't, repeat steps 1 and 2 until they do.

Step 3: Reduce management

The best time to start reducing management is after at least one successful week of no accidents in the house. This means we have been consistently bringing our puppy to their potty area, rewarding all good toileting and learnt our puppy's potty cues.

From there we can be confident that we can start giving them more space. Here's how to start:

After puppy uses their potty area, we reward them, then bring them back inside. We do not need to keep them on leash, in a puppy-proofed space or under our extra watchful eye for about an hour. After the hour is up, we will want to tighten our management again until their next potty break.

Here's a rough guide that can help you reduce your management slowly.

Week one of no accidents: Puppy gets 1 hour of free time then back to managing until the next potty break.

Week two of no accidents: Puppy gets 1.5-2 hours of free time, then back to managing until the next potty break.

Week three of no accidents: Puppy gets 2-3 hours of free time, then back to managing until the next potty break.

All the while, you will want to continue encouraging and prompting potty cues like ringing a doorbell when they need to go outside. House training
is only successful if we can maintain tight management for the first few weeks. I know it can seem daunting at first, but you will fall into a steady routine with your puppy. Before you know it, they will be letting you know when they need to go.

1-2-3
for house training

STEP 1

Management by
preventing
accidents from
happening

STEP 2

Reward your puppy
for going in the
right place

STEP 3

**Loosen
management** after
a successful week
of no accidents

Conclusion

- Use a variety of management options such as a puppy-proof space, keeping puppy on leash or having them on your lap to prevent accidents in the house.

- Provide a legal potty area if puppy will be alone for longer than they can "hold it".

- Reward your puppy for going in the right spot.

- Reduce your management and give puppy more free time after a week of no accidents inside.

- Clean up all accidents with a deodorizer.

- Do not punish after an accident.

NOTES

CHAPTER
SEVEN

Alone Time Training

Alone Time Training

It's not too surprising that, after the 2020 pandemic started, some of the questions asked most by clients deal with alone time training. It has come to many people's attention that their dog or puppy struggles with being alone. This is why I call it alone time training; it requires training.

There are dogs that seem to simply "train themselves" or have no issues being left alone. There are a few reasons for this including; any prep done by the breeder and a puppy's genetics.

Separation anxiety is a genetic anxiety disorder. This may come as a surprise to many pet parents because we are often told that we are the cause to our dog's separation anxiety. Whether it's a friend, a dog park goer, a breeder or the internet, we are made to feel guilty about how we raise our pup. To open this chapter, let's start with some myth busting!

Myth #1: Don't let your puppy sleep with you.
If you have been told this, you are not alone. As a certified separation anxiety trainer, I have found that almost all my clients were given this advice from someone. Often this myth is repeated by a friend or family member; but even professionals such as dog trainers and veterinarians still recommend keeping your puppy in a separate space at night.

Many dogs sleep with their guardians. Many dogs are allowed on furniture and the majority of these dogs do not have separation anxiety. If this was a true cause, most dogs would have separation anxiety.

Sleeping with your puppy is lovely. It's also a great way to get some sleep, versus having them in their crate. Ultimately, where your puppy sleeps is up to you. You have to do what works for you and your puppy.

Myth #2: Puppies must be crate trained to prevent separation anxiety. Crate training is undeniably a useful skill to teach. There might be a point in your puppy's life where they will need to stay in a crate, for example while traveling or for vet care. However, crate training will not prevent separation anxiety. Separation anxiety is genetic. Many dogs with whom I have worked with over the years, also experience confinement anxiety, which can make the symptoms of separation anxiety worse.

Crate training is often the first piece of advice given to a pet parent when a puppy has a hard time being left alone. Crate training will not prevent separation anxiety. Crate training is not always an easy task. This difficulty is not the guardian's fault or the result of the puppy being manipulative or stubborn. Some puppies genuinely have a hard time being confined, and pet parents are not equipped to handle the work load.

If you are struggling with alone time training, or crate training, know that you are not alone. This portion of the chapter is to help rid you of the guilt you may feel, that you "ruined" your puppy. I promise you, you didn't.

Myth #3: Getting another pet will help.
I have worked with dogs who felt much more comfortable being alone with the presence of another animal. However, these dogs are few and far between. I do not suggest adding another animal to your household unless it has been well thought out and you are ready for the added responsibility.

Myth #4: Coddling your puppy will cause separation anxiety.
This myth is one of the more popular myths I see online.

If you follow me on social media, you know how I feel about it. We are often made to feel guilty that we caused all kinds of behaviour issues in our dogs. Separation anxiety is the one I see most often. Here's the thing; we didn't get a dog to keep them in a corner, in a crate or to ignore them half the day. We got a dog to be our friend and companion. Most dogs are "spoiled" by their guardians; by "spoiled", I mean they are well loved, allowed on beds and couches, and cuddle with their guardians. The majority of these dogs are totally fine.

If coddling your puppy caused separation anxiety, nearly every dog would suffer from it. However, they don't. What is really important when you get advice from anyone, even a trainer, is to think critically about it.

Unfortunately, we still have a long way to go when it comes to dispelling myths about separation anxiety. I hope this section has helped clarify some of it and removed any guilt you may feel.

Alone Time Space

Ideally, new guardians would take some time off from work or other obligations to help acclimate puppies to their new homes and progressively get them comfortable with being left alone. Alone time training is a process.

But in any cade, there are a few things we can do to help our puppy feel more comfortable in their alone time space. This space is where puppy will hang out when we are not home, or when we cannot supervise them like when we are showering.

An alone time space can be:
- A dog crate
- A puppy-proofed room
- A puppy playpen

Their alone time space should include:
- A comfortable bed
- A bowl of water
- A variety of food toys including puzzle feeders, lickimats and a stuffed kong
- Appropriate play toys and chews
- A suitable potty area (see house training on page 94 for more details)

I never feel comfortable suggesting withholding water from a dog, especially a young puppy. It's a misconception that it might set your puppy back with house training. They'll drink water, then need to pee. It's definitely possible, and thats why we will set up a suitable potty area.

Puppies can only hold themselves for a short period of time. If they will be alone for longer then 1-2 hours (depending on age), we need to give them a proper potty area until they have been fully housetrained.

Keep in mind that you don't need to use a crate if you are not comfortable, or if your puppy is having a hard time with it. Any puppy-proofed space like a room or playpen works well.

Crate Training

Crate training is a process that is best done slowly. Our goal is to train our puppy to feel comfortable in this space. In order to move forward with our training, we need to ensure our puppy is comfortable. Our puppy sets the pace.

Part 1: Creating positive experiences with the crate

During this first phase, we will begin to create positive experiences to the crate. It will be best not to enclose our puppy in the crate until you have practiced this part a few times.

Step 1: The crate is Disneyland!
Hide a few treats inside the crate (under blankets, in the corners...etc). Then let your puppy discover the treats on their own. You can sit in the room with them and simply wait for them to sniff out the treats. This gives the illusion that the crate is so much fun, like Disneyland!

Step 2: Feed your puppy a stuffed kong or bully stick while in the crate.
This is step 2 because we want our puppy to willingly go in their crate without hesitation or fear. You do not need to feed all of their meals or favourite chews in the crate but doing it a few times will help create those positive experiences.

** Note: I don't recommend closing the door yet, as this may cause your puppy to hesitate to go in. Slow and steady wins the race.

Part 2: Teach puppy to go in on cue

Once you have completed part 1 and your puppy happily walks in their crate without hesitation, we can teach them to go in on cue.

Step 1: Guide your puppy into the crate using a treat. Reward when they go inside and continue to feed 3 to 4 treats as they continue to stay there. (Let your puppy exit as they wish.)

Step 2: Pretend to have a treat in your hand, and guide your puppy into the crate. Give 3 to 4 treats as they continue to stay inside. As always, let your puppy exit if they wish.

Step 3: Add your cue; "in your crate" or "go to bed". Then guide your puppy into their crate as needed. Feed 3 to 4 treats once they go in.

Part 3: Closing the door

Step 1: Close the door half way and feed 3 to 4 treats as your puppy stays inside. If your puppy gets spooked and tries to exit, let them exit. You can make this step easier by simply touching the door instead of trying to close it. We want our puppy to feel comfortable, not cornered. Repeat this step 10 times.

Step 2: Close the door completely and feed 3 to 4 treats to your puppy. Then open the door and let them exit if they wish. If they stay inside, close the door again, and feed 3 to 4 treats. Repeat this step 10 times.

Step 3: Close the latch and feed 3 to 4 treats. Repeat this step 10 times.

Part 4: Increase the amount of time inside the crate

If we took our time in the first 3 sections of crate training, our puppy should:
• Willingly and happily go in their crate
• Go inside on cue
• Be comfortable with the door closed

If the above doesn't sound like your puppy, you will need to continue working on the previous parts of crate training before you start here. Skipping these steps, or going too quickly will only slow you down in part 4.

Crate training rules:
- Only increase how long your puppy is in their crate if they show no signs of stress.
- If your puppy shows signs of stress, let them out and take note of context. (Was it too long? Did they need to go out? Did we move too fast?)
- Mix easier durations with the harder ones. For example, if your puppy is okay with 1 minute, you may want to try 2 or 3 minutes. If all goes well, I would do 1 minute again before moving to 5 minutes.

Next, we will go over how to get your puppy started on being left alone. This next part works well if you have completed the first parts of the crate training process. If you opted out of crate training and are using a puppy-proofed room, you can start alone time training.

Alone Time Training

To start, you will need:
- a puppy-proofed space (see page 81 for the setup)
- a camera (your computer/tablet/old phone work fine)
- a timer
- and a print out of the progress sheet (see page 117)

You will assess your puppy's starting point. To do so, set up your camera to watch your puppy while they are alone. Ideally, you would be watching live. Applications such as FaceTime and Zoom work well, and let you watch from your phone.

Bring your puppy into their alone time space (or crate) and leave, closing the door behind you. Then start your timer. You will now observe your puppy while they are alone.

Do they:

- eat their kong?
- play with their toys?
- lay down on their bed?
- or explore their space?

If yes, continue watching them on camera. The first time being left alone should be capped at 5-10 minutes, even if it's going well. It's best to end on a positive note!

You can make the next sessions a little longer. I suggest increasing by 5 to 10 minute intervals if your puppy is comfortable. Remember to set up their space so that they are safe, they have toys to keep them busy, and they have a potty area if they will be alone for longer then they can hold it.

What if it doesn't go well?

It might not have gone well if your puppy:

- scratches at the door
- whines, barks, howls
- or paces around, looking for you

Take note of how long you were gone when the signs of stress started and come right back.

If your puppy had trouble, don't continue pushing them or make them "cry it out". This will not make being alone a positive experience and might make things worse. While some protesting is normal, panic is not. The goal is to gradually expose your puppy to being alone and is best done at their pace.

If your puppy had a hard time during your first alone time training session, you will need to break it down into smaller steps. Here's how you can do that:

- Practice multiple short absences in a row (example: leaving and coming right back).
- Go to the door without leaving, play with the door handle, play with your keys, grab your bag...etc.
- If your puppy starts to whine at 10 seconds, practice leaving for 5 seconds.
- Provide a tasty chew or kong to make the experience more positive.

Use the following system to rate your puppy's reaction. This will help you determine what your next step should be.

 No signs of stress. Seems happy and relaxed. **Increase duration by 5 to 10 minutes**

 Light signs of stress: some whining, pacing or lightly scratching the door. Does not escalate. **Make next session easier before increasing.**

 Increased signs of stress: barking, whining and howling, non stop pacing, jumping or scratching at the door: **Stop and give them a break. Make the next session at least 50% easier.**

Your puppy sets the pace. As much as we want them to be able to handle 1-2 hours right away, this is not the case for most puppies. Exposure to being left alone must be done gradually. Ensuring your puppy's comfort and well being is of the highest importance!

Separation Anxiety

Separation anxiety is a panic disorder that affects dogs of any age, including puppies. The most important thing to know about separation anxiety is that the cause is genetic. Providing love and safety to your puppy will not cause or worsen separation anxiety. Using punitive training methods (like bark collars), ignoring your puppy or letting them "cry it out" can actually make separation anxiety worse.

The following does not necessarily indicate separation anxiety:
- Your puppy cries at night when alone in their crate
- Your puppy follows you everywhere
- Your puppy is "clingy" and wants to always be in your lap
- Your puppy barks for your attention

Signs of separation anxiety: when alone, your puppy might...
- Howl, cry or whine (intermittently or non-stop)
- Have diarrhea or pee multiple times
- Scratch or bite at the door
- Breathe rapidly (panting)
- Tremble or shake
- Excessively drool
- Turn in circles or pace, looking for you
- Refuse to eat food or treats

These are just some of the many signs of stress observed in dogs who suffer from separation anxiety. Some of these signs can come from something other than separation anxiety such as boredom, incomplete house training, or watchdog barking.

If you suspect your puppy has separation anxiety, the first thing to do is to suspend absences, making sure your puppy is never alone. This will help prevent your puppy from rehearsing alone time anxieties and keep their stress to a minimum. The less experience they have with their anxiety, the better! Then it would be best to reach out to a certified separation anxiety trainer (CSAT) and your veterinary team to help get you started on a personalized training protocol.

Separation anxiety training can help any dog who suffers when alone. With a proper desensitization protocol, many dogs learn to be comfortable with being alone. There's always hope!

Alone time checklist:

Bring puppy out to potty

Play or go for a walk to burn energy

Set up puppy space with toys and puzzle feeders

Ensure puppy has access to fresh water

Set up camera

Print out alone time training log

Have the timer ready to go

COMMON SIGNS OF STRESS:

- Cries, howls or barks non-stop or intermittently
- Destructive to exits such as doors or windows
- Nervous pee
- Diarrhea
- Paces looking for you
- Licks nose
- Ears pulled back
- Ears up (alert)
- Panting
- Yawns
- Hyper salivation
- Trembles
- Blinks eyes rapidly
- Suddenly sniffing the ground
- Hyper vigilant

Alone Time Training Log

Date	Last Potty Break	Time Alone	Reaction	Notes

Reaction: Increase Lower before increasing Make next session 50% easier

NOTES

Thank you

for your trust in me, and for allowing me to help guide you in raising your new puppy. Your support allows me to continue providing accessible training resources to families all over the world. I couldn't do it without you!

Katherine Davidson

CERTIFIED DOG TRAINER

www.doginspired.ca

PUPPY LIFE SKILLS
ONLINE

ON DEMAND - AVAILABLE WORLDWIDE!

The course includes detailed handouts and tutorial videos to help guide you through the training process. It covers puppy life skills, socialization, resource guarding prevention and alone time training.

SIGN UP TODAY TO GET STARTED

USE PROMOCODE "EBOOK" FOR 25% OFF

HTTPS://ACADEMY.DOGINSPIRED.CA

EXTRA RESOURCES

WEBSITES:

- https://academy.doginspired.ca

- https://www.academyfordogtrainers.com

- https://karenpryoracademy.com

- https://malenademartini.com

BOOKS:

- Doggie Language by Lili Chin

- Culture Clash by Jean Donaldson

- Separation Anxiety in Dogs by Malena DeMartini-Price Puppy

- Start Right by Kenneth M. Martin and Debbie

- Life Skills For Puppies by by Helen Zulch, Daniel Mills, et al.

CONTACT US:

www.doginspired.ca

info@doginspired.ca

Made in the USA
Coppell, TX
14 February 2022

73281184R00070